THE NAVAJOS

BY LIZ SONNEBORN

CONSULTANT: MONTY ROESSEL
EXECUTIVE DIRECTOR, ROUGH ROCK COMMUNITY SCHOOL,
CHINLE, ARIZONA

LERNER PUBLICATIONS COMPANY

MINNEAPOLIS

ABOUT THE COVER IMAGE: The humanlike figures on this woven rug are Yei. These powerful spirit beings are an important element of Navajo beliefs.

PHOTO ACKNOWLEDGMENTS:
© Peabody Museum, Harvard University Photo 985-27-10/58876 T3946.1, pp. 1, 3, 4, 14, 22, 30, 41, 44; © Kevin Fleming/CORBIS, pp. 5, 38, 46, 47, 48; Josef Muench Collection, Cline Library, Northern Arizona University, p. 6; Library of Congress, pp. 7, 19, 23, 24, 25, 35; Charles and Grace Herring Collection, Cline Library, Northern Arizona University, p. 8; © Richard Cummins/CORBIS, p. 9; © Bettmann/CORBIS, pp. 10, 42; © Danny Lehman/CORBIS, p. 12; © David Muench/CORBIS, p. 15; Marilyn Angel Wynn/Nativestock.com, pp. 16, 27, 31; Mary May Bailey Collection, Cline Library Northern Arizona University, p. 17; © Christie's Images/CORBIS, p. 18; Arizona Historical Society Tucson, p. 28 (both); Florence Barker Collection, Cline Library, Northern Arizona University, p. 32; NAU General Photograph Collection, Cline Library, Northern Arizona University, p. 33; © North Wind Picture Archives, p. 34; Philip Johnston Collection, Cline Library, Northern Arizona University, pp. 36, 39; © CORBIS, pp. 37, 40; © Ric Ergenbright/CORBIS, p. 43; © Catherine Karnow/CORBIS, p. 45; © Dave G. Houser/CORBIS, p. 49; Elijah Blair Collection, Cline Library, Northern Arizona University, p. 50.

Front Cover: © Werner Forman/Art Resource, NY

Lerner Publications Company
A division of Lerner Publishing Group
241 First Avenue North
Minneapolis, MN 55401 U.S.A.

Website address: www.lernerbooks.com

Library of Congress Cataloging-in-Publication Data

Sonneborn, Liz.
  The Navajos / by Liz Sonneborn.
      p.   cm. — (Native American histories)
  Includes bibliographical references and index.
  ISBN-13: 978-0-8225-2445-8 (lib. bdg. : alk. paper)
  ISBN-10: 0-8225-2445-7 (lib. bdg. : alk. paper)
  1. Navajo Indians—History. 2. Navajo Indians—Social life and customs. I. Title. II. Series.
E99.N3S66 2007
979.1004'9726—dc22   2004011628

Manufactured in the United States of America
1 2 3 4 5 6 – BP – 12 11 10 09 08 07

CONTENTS

CHAPTER 1

THE GLITTERING WORLD

LONG AGO, ALL CREATURES LIVED IN THE BLACK WORLD.

But they could not get along with one another there, so they decided to leave. They moved first through the Blue World and then through the Yellow World. Finally, they entered the Glittering World—a place where all things were in balance. In this world, humans and animals could live together in harmony.

This is one version of the creation story told for centuries by the Navajo people. The Navajos call themselves the Diné. This name means "the people." They are one group of the peoples native to North America. These peoples are often called American Indians or Native Americans. The Navajos make up the largest Indian tribe, or group, in the United States. Most Navajos live in New Mexico, Arizona, and Utah.

Generations of Navajo people have passed down stories of the Glittering World. Navajos like Peter Martin *(right)* tell these tales to their children and grandchildren.

The rugged and beautiful landscape of the American Southwest
is the heart of the Navajo homeland.

Like the creatures in the story, the ancestors of
the Navajo people made a great journey.
Hundreds of years ago, these people lived in
present-day Canada. Later, they began traveling
southward, possibly in search of food. By about
A.D. 1400, they had settled in what would become
the southwestern United States.

A NEW HOME

In the north, the Navajos' ancestors had been hunters. They had traveled from place to place, looking for wild animals and plants. In their southwestern homeland, they found another way to get food. They learned to farm corn, beans, squash, melons, and other crops from the Pueblos, another southwestern Indian group.

Corn planted by Navajo farmers grows in a canyon. Also called maize, corn is sacred to Navajos.

The Navajos also started building a new type of house. They had once lived in dwellings made from animal skins draped over a wooden frame. But in the Southwest, there were fewer large animals to hunt for these skins. Navajo families depended more on logs, bark, and leaves to build their homes instead. These houses were called hogans.

A Navajo family outside their hogan. Some hogans were made of earth and wood, while others, like this one, used stone.

The sun rises over the Navajo homeland. Navajo traditions deeply respect the sun and its power.

Each hogan had one large room surrounded by six or eight walls. A hole in one wall was used as a door. It always faced the east, so that the people inside could see the rising sun each morning.

Relatives usually built their hogans close to one another. That way, they could work together to raise crops. When a man and woman married, they went to live near the woman's family.

Every Navajo person belonged to a clan. Clans were larger groups of Navajos who considered themselves especially closely related. Children belonged to their mother's clan.

The Navajos lived in small communities spread over a large area in the Southwest. Sometimes local leaders had influence over several settlements. But the entire tribe did not recognize any one leader. No one spoke for all the Navajos.

Mothers helped teach their children about Navajo life.

THE KINAALDÁ CEREMONY

The Kinaaldá celebrates a Navajo girl's move into womanhood. The ceremony lasts for four days. People sing, pray, and dress the girl in special clothes. Older women talk to the girl about how to be strong and responsible so that she will become a good Navajo woman. The Kinaaldá is a happy occasion. It brings the girl the blessings of her friends and family and ensures her well-being in the future. The Kinaaldá ceremony is still held in modern Navajo communities.

SEEKING HOZHO

One thing that connected all Navajo people was their religious beliefs. These beliefs drew on the idea of *hozho*—a state of complete harmony and beauty. Hozho was fragile. It was always threatened by disorder in the world.

To restore weakened hozho, the Navajos performed ceremonies that often lasted for days.

Holy people led these ceremonies, singing songs
and reciting prayers. Some were held to cure the
sick. For instance, the Night Way is a healing
ceremony that took nine days and nights. It
involved more than three hundred songs.

Healers often used sandpaintings to cure their
patients. Sandpaintings were designs formed from
colored sand and other natural materials.

Navajo sandpaintings are very sacred. Healers use carefully prepared
dishes of colored sand and powders to create their paintings.

Navajo healers made these designs on the floors of hogans. Sandpaintings often showed the spirits that are told of in old Navajo stories. These spirits protected the Navajo people, allowing them to do well in the Glittering World.

CHAPTER 2

MEETING STRANGERS

IN THE EARLY 1500s, after the Navajos had come to the Southwest, an army of strangers arrived. These men rode on tall horses and wore heavy, metal armor that gleamed in the hot sun. They were soldiers from Spain. They were the first non-Indians in the Southwest.

The Spanish soldiers were looking for gold. They had heard rumors that the villages of the Pueblos were filled with the precious metal. Even the buildings were said to be made of gold.

In 1540, the Spaniards attacked the Pueblo village of Zuni. The Zuni Pueblos fought hard. But their wooden weapons were no match for the Spaniards' guns. The Spanish soldiers won the battle. To their disappointment, however, the stories about Pueblo gold turned out to be false. The Spanish army soon left Zuni.

This Navajo rock painting in Arizona shows the arrival of the Spanish, on horseback, in the Southwest.

But Spain continued to send soldiers and settlers to the Southwest. They took control of several other Pueblo villages and forced the defeated Pueblo people to work for them. The Navajos saw what the Spaniards were doing to the Pueblos. Navajo people were suspicious of these newcomers and did their best to avoid them.

LEARNING FROM THE SPANISH

The Navajos distrusted the Spaniards. But they were pleased with some of the things that they

A painting on an animal skin shows a battle between the Pueblo people and the Spanish. The Spanish soldiers carry long guns.

The arrival of the Spanish brought great sadness to Native Americans. But the Spanish also brought sheep and horses. Sheepherding remains important to Navajo life.

brought to the Southwest. The Navajos were impressed by Spanish guns. Navajo men could use these weapons in case of war with other Native American groups. They could also use them if they needed to hunt. But even more useful were the Spaniards' horses and sheep. The Indians of the Southwest had never seen these animals before. Yet they quickly became a central part of Navajo life.

Navajos began using horses to cross the wide deserts and canyons of the Southwest.

Horses allowed the Navajos to travel long distances faster than ever before. On horseback, Navajo traders went to new lands and met new trading partners. They could also visit faraway Navajo villages. And warriors found that they could fight their enemies better when they took horses into battle.

Sheep were just as useful. The meat of these animals made a tasty stew that soon became a favorite Navajo food. Navajo women spun yarn from the sheep's wool. They then wove the yarn into beautiful blankets for their families. Navajo people often wore these blankets draped around their shoulders.

Navajo women weave blankets on large looms. The sheep that probably provided the wool stand on a ledge above.

TENDING THE HERDS

Navajos took great pride in their sheep-herding skills, and the herds were very important to Navajo society. A large, healthy herd provided the herder's family with meat, milk, and wool. It also showed friends and relatives that the herder was a hard worker and a good person. Respected herders had to know how to feed and care for their animals. They also had to perform rituals and say special prayers to keep their sheep safe from harm.

Navajos built large herds of horses and sheep. Sometimes they traded with Pueblos and other Indian peoples for these animals. Navajo raiders also stole them from other Indians' villages.

Sometimes Navajos raided Spanish towns for animals and food. The Spaniards, in turn, attacked Navajo settlements. Spanish soldiers deeply angered and saddened the Navajos by seizing hundreds of men, women, and children. They sold these Navajo captives into slavery.

These attacks continued over hundreds of years. Finally, in 1821, Spain lost control over its Southwestern territory. This land became part of the country of Mexico. The Navajo people welcomed the end of this tragic period. But soon, they faced a new challenge. U.S. soldiers and settlers wanted to take Navajo land and make it their own.

CHAPTER 3

THE LONG WALK

IN 1846, THE UNITED STATES WENT TO WAR AGAINST MEXICO. Two years later, Mexico lost the Mexican-American War. Mexico had to give the United States about half of its territory. This territory included Navajo lands in what would later become New Mexico and Arizona. Soon large numbers of American settlers began moving onto Navajo land. The Navajos also had to deal with U.S. soldiers who were sent to protect the settlers.

FIGHTING U.S. SOLDIERS

As the years passed, tensions between the Navajos and the Americans grew. Before long, many Navajo people decided that they had had enough of these outsiders on their lands. In 1860, Manuelito and Barboncito, two highly respected Navajos, led a force of one thousand Navajo men. They attacked Fort Defiance, a U.S. Army post on Navajo territory.

MANUELITO spent his life defending the Navajos against enemies. As a young man, he was a respected warrior. He fought the Americans. To the suffering Navajo people, Manuelito became a symbol of hope and resistance.

The warriors nearly captured the fort. But the U.S. soldiers had better weapons. They defeated the Navajos.

The U.S. government came up with a new plan for dealing with the Navajos. In the fall of 1862, Brigadier General James Carleton was put in command of soldiers in the Southwest. Carleton's job was to move the Indians living there onto reservations. Reservations were small pieces of land given to Indian tribes by the United States.

At least twenty Navajo warriors were killed in the attack on Fort Defiance (*below*). The U.S. Army used the fort for many years after the attack. This photograph is from 1905.

James Carleton treated the Navajos and other Native Americans very harshly.

On reservations, Carleton, his soldiers, and other U.S. officials controlled almost everything the Indians did. Many U.S. settlers still feared Indian attacks. With the reservation plan, the government hoped to keep Americans safe from Indian attacks. But the plan also gave the United States control over Indian territory in the area. Many Americans thought there was gold on the Navajo homeland.

In April 1863, Carleton met with several Navajo leaders. He said the Navajos had to move to Bosque Redondo, a reservation in what became east-central New Mexico. His troops would hunt down anyone who refused.

In July, soldiers began rounding up Navajos by force. They captured many people and killed others. They destroyed homes, fields, and herds. Facing starvation, thousands of Navajos surrendered as winter approached.

TERRIBLE BATTLES

Navajo healer Eli Gorman shared a story that his father told him about U.S. soldiers rounding up Navajos for Bosque Redondo. "The firing gradually picked up, and soon it sounded like frying, with bullets hitting all over the cave. This went on nearly all afternoon. . . . Men, women, children, young men and girls were all killed on the cliffs. . . . Blood could be seen from the top of the cliffs all the way down to the bottom."

BOSQUE REDONDO

About nine thousand Navajos traveled on foot to Bosque Redondo. Many died during the terrible 250-mile trip. The soldiers shot any Navajos who lagged behind, even if they were old or sick. The trip became known as the Long Walk.

Things grew worse at Bosque Redondo. The reservation was small. There was not enough water, clothing, or farmland for everyone.

Survivors of the Long Walk are crowded together at Fort Sumner. The fort was a military center on the Bosque Redondo reservation.

There was too little wood for fuel and shelter. Hungry, cold, and exhausted, many more Navajos died of disease at Bosque Redondo.

Some U.S. officials were horrified by the suffering of the Navajos. Others were outraged at how much the United States was spending to house them at Bosque Redondo. The government fired Carleton. In 1868, two officials arrived to talk with the Navajos. They suggested sending the

This young boy (*left*) and Navajo warrior (*right*) were two of the captives at Bosque Redondo.

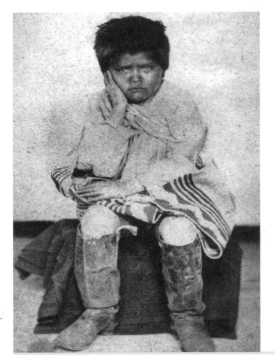

Navajo people to a reservation in Texas or in the Indian Territory (later called Oklahoma).

But the Navajo leaders said no. They wanted only one thing—to return to their homeland. And after a few months, the officials agreed. They signed a treaty with the Navajos. They gave the tribe 3.5 million acres of land in northeastern Arizona and northwestern New Mexico. This new reservation was only one-fourth the size of their original lands. Even so, the Navajo people were glad. After years of misery at Bosque Redondo, they were going home at last.

CHAPTER 4

BUILDING A NATION

IN THE SUMMER OF 1868, the Navajos began another long, hard journey—this time to their new reservation. As the Navajos came home, they were deeply saddened by their many losses. More than half of the people who had been forced onto the Long Walk never saw their homeland again. And four years away had changed those who did return. Before the Long Walk, the Navajos had lived in many small, independent communities. They had not thought of themselves as one people.

But at Bosque Redondo, they had developed a new sense of what it meant to be Navajo. They had learned that they must depend on one another. As the Navajos came home, they were determined to work together to build a new life.

MORE CHANGES

The first years on the reservation were difficult. Bad weather caused crops to fail. Many Navajo people went hungry. And Indian enemies often attacked the reservation.

In 1874, Navajo leaders visited Washington, D.C., to talk about the 1868 treaty. The group included Manuelito and his wife, Juanita *(front row, center)*.

Non-Indian visitors on the Navajo reservation gather for a photo.
With them are Navajos Hosteen Yazzie (*back row, in hat*)
and Hazel and Anna Fairfield (*front row, right*).

Navajos also faced the challenge of dealing
with non-Indians more than ever before. The
U.S. government hired agents to run the
reservations. Sometimes the Navajos and the
agents did not get along.

Missionaries came to live with the Navajo
people too. These religious workers tried to
convert the Navajos to Christianity. Some
Navajos became Christians. But others continued
to follow their traditional religious beliefs.

The United States sent teachers to the Navajo reservation as well. Teachers at government-run schools taught Navajo children to speak English. They also introduced their students to non-Indian ways.

Most Navajo parents did not like these schools. They wanted to educate their children the way they always had. Navajo children had always learned by watching adults. In this way, they learned about the work they would do when they grew up.

Three Navajo girls wear the uniform of their boarding school at Fort Defiance. Students in boarding schools live at school rather than at home. Many Navajos did not like these government-run schools.

DOING BUSINESS

In addition to agents, missionaries, and teachers, non-Indian traders came to the reservation. They built trading posts where customers could exchange some goods for others. Traders offered the Navajos metal pots, cloth, and flour in return for crops and wool.

The Navajos also traded their handmade woolen blankets. Non-Indians were eager to buy these beautiful and colorful weavings.

The Hubbell Trading Post was built in 1878. It is still open for business.

A silversmith carefully shapes silver that has been softened by the fire.

Traders wanted Navajo women to make rugs, which sold for high prices. They also urged Navajo men to take up silversmithing. Tribal silversmiths used silver and turquoise stones to make necklaces, bracelets, and rings. In time, Navajo craftspeople became famous for their goods.

Still another change in Navajo life came in the 1920s. During those years, valuable oil was discovered on the reservation. Oil is used for fuel.

The U.S. governement wanted to use this oil.
U.S. officials urged the Navajos to form a tribal
council. U.S. leaders also helped choose the
members of this council. They picked people
who would be willing to make deals with oil
companies. The group was not popular with
many Navajos at first. But eventually it became
an important part of the tribal government.
These leaders were the first officials to speak for
the entire tribe.

An oil rig stands out against the flat landscape of the Navajo homeland.
Rigs are used for drilling into the earth and removing underground oil.

The new tribal council made many important decisions for the Navajo people.

In the 1930s, the tribal council faced a tough problem. The U.S. government wanted the Navajos to make their herds smaller. Thousands of sheep had eaten so much of the reservation's grass that the dirt below was bare. The land was being destroyed as wind and water carried away rich soil.

Instead of reducing herds, the Navajos asked the government to make the reservation bigger. Then their sheep would have more grazing land.

Navajos fiercely resisted having their herds made smaller. They said it would hurt their economy. Sheep are also closely tied to Navajo culture. Families still herd and take care of sheep and lambs.

Over the years, the United States had increased the reservation's size several times already. By the 1930s, it was about one-fifth of the size of Arizona. But this time, the United States refused to expand the reservation. Instead, U.S. officials went to the reservation to force the Navajos to reduce their herds. They bought some animals but paid very little for them. They killed other animals. The rotting bodies of sheep soon covered the land. Navajos were furious and saddened.

GOING TO WAR

Navajos were angry about the government's reducing their herds. But even so, they strongly supported the United States in World War II (1939–1945). Many signed up to fight. About 3,600 Navajo men and women joined the U.S. military during the war.

The U.S. military sent officers to the Navajo reservation to recruit soldiers to fight in World War II.

Some these volunteers were the Code Talkers. These men served in the South Pacific. They passed along secret messages using a code created from the Navajo language. The enemy tried to crack the code, but never did. The Code Talkers became American heroes for their bravery. In 2001, President George W. Bush awarded twenty-nine Code Talkers the Congressional Gold Medal.

CODE TALKING

The Navajo Code Talkers spelled out messages using a secret alphabet. They used a different Navajo word to stand for each letter. For instance, the word *wol-la-chee* (meaning "ant") stood for the letter *A*, *klizzie* (goat) represented *G*, and *a-keh-di-glini* (victor) represented *V*.

CHAPTER 5

THE MODERN NAVAJOS

AFTER WORLD WAR II, the Navajos worked to build a modern American Indian nation. This task brought new difficulties. The tribal government faced several problems with leaders who broke rules. The Navajo Nation also dealt with an ongoing disagreement with the Hopis. The Hopis are a branch of the Pueblo peoples. They believed that some land on the Navajo reservation belonged to them. A legal battle between the two groups forced about three thousand Navajo families to give up their land and leave their homes

But despite these troubles, the Navajo population has grown steadily. About 175,000 Navajos live on the reservation. Another 100,000 Navajos live in other parts of the United States. Many have homes in towns bordering the reservation. They also live in large western cities.

ANNIE DODGE WAUNEKA helped strengthen the Navajo Nation. In 1951, she was the first woman elected to the tribal council. She also served as chairwoman of the Navajo government's health committee for thirty years. She worked hard to improve the health of her people. In 1963, she became the first American Indian to receive the Presidential Medal of Freedom.

A Navajo woman wears beautiful turquoise and silver jewelry. Navajo legends say that turquoise can guard against harm.

EARNING A LIVING

Making ends meet is a struggle for many reservation residents. Some Navajos, especially older people, are very poor. They often live in houses without running water or electricity.

A few Navajos still tend sheep, but herds are usually small. Others weave rugs or make silver jewelry for sale. Master weavers and silversmiths continue to teach young Navajos about these arts. But most Navajos work in less traditional jobs, such as construction and housecleaning. Many have trouble finding any work at all.

NAVAJO ARTS AND CRAFTS

The Navajo Arts and Crafts Enterprise sells rugs, silver jewelry, and other work made by Navajo craftspeople. The enterprise dates back to the 1940s. It has grown into a 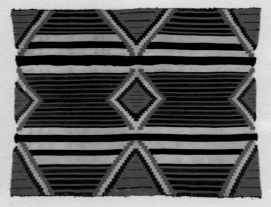 multimillion-dollar business. It runs stores throughout the Navajo reservation and in nearby towns.

The tribe makes some money by selling the reservation's natural resources. These resources include coal, oil, and wood. But these business deals do not create very many jobs for Navajos. There are not very many employers on the reservation. The tribal council has tried to bring outside companies to Navajo lands. But because of bad roads and a lack of electricity and water, few businesses want to move there.

Tourism, however, has thrived. People from all over the world come to see the reservation's natural beauty and historic sites. Navajo businesspeople run tour groups and hotels for these visitors. Tourists can pay to stay overnight in a traditional hogan. Most modern Navajo families live in houses. But some Navajo people also still use hogans as homes or as places for religious ceremonies.

Many Navajo businesspeople run small tourism companies. This one offers horseback tours of Monument Valley in Arizona.

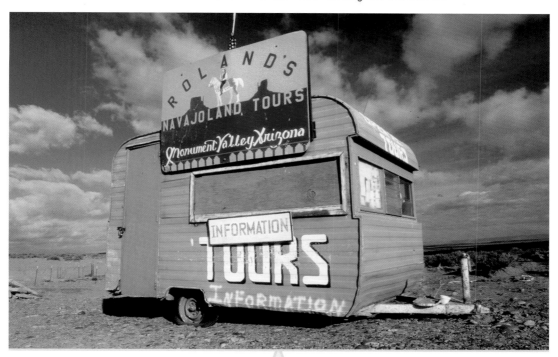

KEEPING THEIR CULTURE ALIVE

The Navajo people hope to make a bright future for their children. They are working hard to improve the reservation's schools. Many of these schools teach Navajo history and culture. They also offer classes in the Navajo language, since most families speak English at home. Each year, more Navajo students go to college. Diné College is a popular choice. This four-year college is run by the Navajo Nation.

A Navajo teacher helps a young student with her schoolwork. Navajo teachers often have a close relationship with their students. They see them almost as family members.

A group of young men play basketball. This sport is one of the most popular pastimes in modern Navajo communities, both for the players and for the audience.

Many Navajo students are talented basketball players. Their high school teams have won several Arizona state championships. Players' friends and neighbors cheer them on all the way. And most Navajos love rodeos almost as much as basketball. A rodeo takes place somewhere on the reservation nearly every summer weekend. On the Fourth of July, the Arizona town of Window Rock hosts a huge rodeo. The event attracts thousands of visitors.

Window Rock is also the home of the Navajo tribal government. The government is led by a president and vice president elected by the Navajo people. The Navajo Nation Council makes laws for the reservation. The council is made up of eighty-eight elected representatives. It meets in a hogan-shaped building that is decorated with scenes from Navajo history. The Navajo Nation also has its own court system and police force.

Laws passed by the Navajo Nation Council at Window Rock are written in both English and the Navajo language.

R. C. GORMAN is famous for his beautiful paintings. Born in 1931 on the Navajo reservation, Gorman is the son of the artist Carl N. Gorman. R. C. Gorman served in the U.S. Navy before becoming a painter. He has worked in many art forms, including sculpture and printmaking. Gorman's art is in museums around the world.

Since arriving in the Southwest, the Navajo people have faced many challenges. They learned to live in a new place, deal with many strange peoples, and protect themselves from unfamiliar enemies. Coping with a changing world has helped the Navajos grow strong as a people. But their fierce pride in being Navajo is one thing in their lives that has never changed.

THE CHIEF BLANKET

In the 1800s, Navajo weavers became famous for their blankets and rugs. Chief Blankets were especially popular. The Navajos often traded these blankets to other tribes. The finely made Chief Blankets were so valuable that supposedly only tribal leaders (sometimes called chiefs) could afford them.

Using construction paper, you can make your own version of a Chief Blanket.

WHAT YOU NEED:

3 large pieces of construction paper— 1 black, 1 red, and 1 white

ruler

pencil (for marking measurements)

scissors

glue or glue stick

black felt-tip marker

WHAT TO DO:

1. Cut a square out of the black paper. Make each side about 9 inches long.

2. Cut the white paper into four strips. Each strip should be about 1 inch wide and 9 inches long.

3. Glue the white strips to the black paper, leaving about 1 inch between the strips.

4. Cut four squares out of the red paper. The sides of each square should be about 3½ inches long.

5. Glue one red square diagonally in the middle of the black paper to make a diamond shape.

6. Cut two of the other red squares in half to create four triangles. Glue one triangle in the middle of each side of the black paper, with the points touching the points of the center square.

7. Cut the last red square into four smaller triangles. Glue one in each corner of the black paper.

8. Use the black marker to draw lines or crosses on the red diamond and triangles.

PLACES TO VISIT

Hubbell Trading Post National Historic Site

Ganado, Arizona

(928) 755-3475

http://www.nps.gov/hutr

The Hubbell Trading Post is the oldest trading post on the Navajo reservation. It was established in 1878.

Monument Valley Navajo Tribal Park

Monument Valley, Utah

(928) 871-6647

http://www.navajonationparks.org/oldsite/monumentvalley2.htm

This park was established by the Navajo Nation. It is famed for its beautiful landscape. Colorful rock formations dot the valley floor.

Navajo Museum, Library, and Visitor Center

Window Rock, Arizona

(928) 871-7941

http://www.discovernavajo.com/atr_navajomuseum.html

Opened in 1997, this museum presents displays about Navajo life and about other Indian groups. The building is designed to resemble a hogan.

Ned Hatathli Museum

Tsaile, Arizona

(928) 724-6800

http://www.dinecollege.edu

This museum is named after a noted Navajo leader. It has exhibits about Navajo culture and history.

Window Rock Navajo Tribal Park and Veterans Memorial

Window Rock, Arizona

(928) 871-6647

http://www.navajonationparks.org/veteranspark.htm

This park features the famous rock formation Window Rock. Nearby is a monument to Navajos who have served in the U.S. military.

GLOSSARY

American Indian: a member of the peoples native to North America or a person descended from these people. American Indians are also sometimes called Native Americans.

clan: a group of relatives within a tribe

Code Talkers: Navajo soldiers who communicated secret messages during World War II (1939–1945). The Code Talkers used a code based on the Navajo language.

hogan: a traditional Navajo house. Hogans usually have six or eight sides.

hozho: a sense of well-being and harmony valued by the Navajo people. Hozho is a central idea in the Navajo belief system.

Long Walk: the difficult journey the Navajos made on foot in 1864 to Bosque Redondo, a reservation in modern New Mexico

missionaries: people who try to persuade others to adopt their religion

reservation: an area of land set aside by the U.S. government for use by a particular American Indian group

sandpainting: a picture made from colored sand and powdered minerals and used during traditional Navajo healing ceremonies

treaty: a written agreement between two or more nations or groups

tribe: a group of American Indians who share the same language, customs, and religious beliefs

FURTHER READING

Bruchac, Joseph. *The Navajo Long Walk*. Washington, DC: National Geographic, 2002. This book, by a Native American author and a Native American illustrator, tells the tragic story of the Long Walk.

Hucko, Bruce. *A Rainbow at Night: The World in Words and Pictures by Navajo Children*. San Francisco: Chronicle, 1996. Navajo children express themselves through art in this colorful collection.

Morgan, William. *Coyote Tales*. Walnut, CA: Kiva Publishing, 2000. This collection of traditional Navajo stories stars Coyote, a mischievous trickster character.

Roessel, Monty. *Kinaaldá: A Navajo Girl Grows Up*. Minneapolis: First Avenue Editions, 1993. Join Celinda McKelvey as she goes through the important Kinaaldá ceremony.

———. *Songs from the Loom: A Navajo Girl Learns to Weave*. Minneapolis: Lerner Publications Company, 1995. Readers meet a Navajo family and see how the tradition of weaving is passed down through the generations.

Thomson, Peggy. *Katie Henio: Navajo Sheepherder*. New York: Cobblehill Books, 1995. Meet a Navajo woman and her sheep in an introduction to an important part of Navajo history and culture.

WEBSITES

The Discover Navajo Experience
http://www.nativeamericanx.com/discovernavajo
This website offers information on a wide variety of topics in Navajo culture and society.

The Navajo Nation
http://www.navajo.org
The official website of the Navajo Nation offers information on tribal government, current events, and other news.

Navajo Nation Hospitality Enterprise
http://www.explorenavajo.com
The official site of a group founded to organize and promote tourism on the Navajo reservation.

Navajo Times Online
http://www.thenavajotimes.com
This Navajo newspaper presents a range of articles on news, sports, entertainment, and more.

SELECTED BIBLIOGRAPHY

Davis, Mary B., ed. *Native America in the Twentieth Century: An Encyclopedia*. New York: Garland Publishing, 1996.

Hirschfelder, Arlene, and Paulette Molin. *The Encyclopedia of Native American Religions*. New York: Facts on File, 1992.

Hoxie, Frederick, ed. *Encyclopedia of North American Indians*. Boston: Houghton Mifflin, 1996.

Iverson, Peter. *Diné: A History of the Navajos*. Albuquerque: University of New Mexico, 2002.

———. *The Navajo*. New York: Chelsea House, 1990.

Roessell Ruth. *Navajo Stories of the Long Walk Period*. Tsaile, AZ: Navajo Community College Press, 1973.

Sonneborn, Liz. *Chronology of American Indian History*. New York: Facts on File, 2001.

Sturtevant, William C., ed. *Handbook of North American Indians*. Vol. 10. Washington, DC: Smithsonian Institution, 1988.

Waldman, Carl. *Encyclopedia of Native American Tribes*. Rev. ed. New York: Facts on File, 1999.

INDEX